Calm & Peace

Calm & Peace

Highly sought the world over are the benefits to

Calm &

Peace

That is, the calm and peace
that are within one's grasp.

Adrina Green

© Copyright - Adrina Green 2013

All rights reserved. This book is protected by copyright laws. No part of this publication may be reproduced, stored in a retrieval system, or transmitted in any form or by any means, electronic, mechanical, photocopying, recording or otherwise, for commercial gain or profit without written permission from the author. The use of short quotations or occasional page copying for personal or group study is permitted and encouraged.

National Library of Australia
Cataloguing-in-Publication entry

Author:	Green, Adrina
Title:	Calm & Peace / Adrina Green
ISBN:	978-0-9871010-0-6 (pbk.)
Subjects:	Calmness
	Peace
	Quietude
	Emotions – Religious aspects.
Dewey Number:	126

Publisher: Adrina Green
For Worldwide Distribution
Printed in the U.S.A.
For Information on Distributors go to:
calmandpeace.com

© Copyright – Scripture

(CEV) Contemporary English Version, American Bible Society © 1995

(GNB) Good News Bible: Some scriptures are quoted from the *Good News Bible* © 1994 published by the Bible Societies/HarperCollins Publishers Ltd., *UK Good News Bible* © American Bible Society © 1966, 1971, 1976, 1992. Used with permission. Today's English Version, Second edition © 1992

Old Testament, American Bible Society © 1976, 1992

New Testament, American Bible Society © 1966, 1971, 1976, 1992

(NIV) New International Version: Scripture taken from the Holy Bible, New International Version® © 1973, 1978, 1984 by International Bible Society. Used by permission of Zondervan Publishing House. All Rights reserved.

The "NIV" and "New International Version" trademarks are registered in the United States Patent and Trademark Office by the International Bible Society. Use of either trademark requires the permission of the International Bible Society.

(KNJV) New King James Version: Scripture taken from the New King James Version.

Copyright © 1979, 1980, 1982 by Thomas Nelsen, Inc. Used by permission. All rights reserved.

~ *Acknowledgements* ~

I feel privileged to be living in the era of the internet; a time when sourcing information, quality services, and accessing books from just about anywhere in the world is made possible with the touch of a button.

On this occasion, I would like to acknowledge the many generations of writers who have left with us a legacy of written dialogue on calm and peace.

This book has taken six years to complete, and in that time I have spent many hours researching and reading valuable literature from a wide range of sources. To the writers I have quoted in my book, I give particular thanks for their thought-provoking words of wisdom.

I thank WordsRU and Scribendi who source their professional editors from around the globe. Both were careful to connect my work with editors who have specialist degrees in the field in which I am writing. I thank these editors for their valuable input.

~Dedication~

*A gem without sanding and polishing
is just a dull stone.*

I dedicate this book to God, who showed me where in my thinking I could benefit from a little sanding and polishing.

Adrina Green

~ From the Author ~

Since the age of fifteen, I have sought natural alternatives to deal with stress. At the age of thirty-seven, after suffering severe stress-related heart palpitations, I began an even deeper search for answers to a problem that affects the majority of the population. I believe that although life itself is a challenge, our attitude is always a choice, and this belief has become the catalyst for me to turn my life around. I have discovered the value of listening closely to my internal dialogue and controlling it rather than letting it control me. I am benefiting from my notion that *the stress we talk ourselves into is the stress we can talk ourselves out of.* I have also discovered that forgiveness is the key to releasing the pressure valves. Not only are my heart palpitations reducing, but I am also learning how to be calm amid the storms of life. In this book, I openly share my wisdom and insight in the sincere hope that you and others may benefit from them.

Adrina Green

~ *Preface* ~

It is time to throw away the bumper sticker that says "life sucks" and embrace the attitude that "life can be good and getting better"?

Similar to fighters in the ring, we are taught that it is to our advantage to get back up when we are knocked down. In the case of fighters, they study their sport and practice regularly because they prefer to stay on their feet. In life, wisdom and training are available for those who wish to stay alert and manage the punches that inevitably come their way. There are ways to develop a calm and confident inner peace.

Furthermore, calm and peace are victorious when everyday people choose smiles and handshakes instead of scowls and hatred. An even greater victory is won when this calm and peace become contagious.

Annotation: -

*All italicized quotations in the book
were written by the author.*

~ *Contents* ~

Calm & Peace

1

~~~

~~~~

Be Calm
Amid the storm

Challenge and choice

Have you ever wondered whether other people are happier, more at peace, or have a greater passion for life than you do? Or have you ever asked the question, "Am I missing something here?" If your answer is "yes," don't worry; you are not alone.

My uncle was a very distinguished gentleman who was wise and well-loved. In WWII, he played a key role in the British Air Force as part of an elite group selected for high profile missions. He died recently at age 82. I came away from his funeral thinking about two of his famous sayings. One was a conviction about how one should live: "Live as though every day is Christmas day!" he would say. The other was the reply he would give whenever he was asked, "How are you?": "Good—and getting better!" He would always answer this with a smile, no matter how he was feeling.

That afternoon, I sat looking into the sunset and pondered whether I perceived my life as "good and getting better." Did I have a passion for life that included a little bit of Christmas every day? And what was it about Christmas that I would want to have in my life every day? Knowing for sure that it would not be the expense, the harrowing shopping trips, or the inevitable family bickering, I was left with the original meaning of Christmas: "On earth, peace and good will toward men!"[i]

Like everyone, I had always desired to enjoy life and make the most of it, and like most of us, I discovered that I was still open to unforeseen storms, even in the simple pursuit of happiness. I started to suffer heart palpitations in my late thirties. As my stress levels worsened, I read more on the subject and experimented with the answers I found. The advantage of maintaining a calm, confident inner peace in all circumstances soon became apparent.

The first thing I reviewed was the assumption that peace and happiness are mostly controlled by outer circumstances, whether one is living in a peaceful, splendid, and thriving environment, or living under harsh or war-like conditions; whether we are born rich or born poor; and whether the people around us are in a good or a bad mood. I know that some even attribute their mood to the weather; whether it is a gorgeous, sunny day or a miserable, wet one.

In April 2007, Libby Lenton (now Libby Trickett) won five gold medals in the world swimming championships, and having planned her wedding while training for the competition, was married the following week. Did I mention that she was studying to complete a Bachelor of Communications degree at the same time? Fiona Purdon of the Courier Mail was impressed with Libby's ability to balance three major projects at once, and she asked her what her secret was. Libby replied by quoting an unknown author: "Peace doesn't mean to be in a place where there is no trouble or hard work; it is to be in the midst of all these things, and still be calm in your heart."

Inspiration from others

It is easy for people to be calm and happy when the sun is shining and life is cruising, but what about when the roof is flying off and life is stormy? Life's storms can be just as random as real storms; a tornado can hit one house and miss the next. We don't feel so alone when we look around and see others who are facing similar or even tougher experiences. Storms may be frightening, but it is always good advice to remain calm, as storms do pass. Some storms leave trails of destruction that take time and work to repair. The world is full of stories from those who have encountered one of life's storms. Especially compelling are the stories of the challenges faced by the innocent who have been imprisoned, or those facing a physical disability. No matter what the challenge, when people choose calm and courage, they are an inspiration to others by their example and the words they share.

> *Although life is a challenge,*
> *attitude is always a choice.*

Christopher Reeve had a healthy body and a rewarding career as an actor, playing the role of Superman, a "superhero," until an unfortunate horse riding accident left him a quadriplegic. What an extreme contrast between these highs and lows that he was challenged to cope with mentally. His words are inspiring:

> I think a hero is an ordinary individual who finds strength to persevere and endure in spite of overwhelming obstacles ... What I do is based on powers we all have inside us: the ability to endure; the ability to love, to carry on, to make the best of what we have – and you don't have to be a Superman to do it (Christopher Reeve, 1952–2004).

Helen Keller was afflicted with an illness when she was nineteen months old that left her deaf, blind, and mute. She cherished the memory of her first day at a special school, when her teacher held her hand under water and traced the word "water" on her palm. Helen went on to become a writer and social activist, and Winston Churchill called her "the greatest woman of our age." We would do well to heed her words:

> When one door of happiness closes another opens, but often we look so long at the closed door that we do not see the one which has been opened for us … A happy life consists not in the absence, but in the mastery, of hardships (Helen Keller, 1880–1968).

Throughout history, millions of men and women have been forced into prisons or slavery and left with nothing but hope for freedom and peace in their lands. Army captivity manuals teach a soldier, if he is imprisoned, to keep his mind active and his thoughts positive, to take care of his hygiene, and always to have an escape strategy! This may be good advice for soldiers, but not all prisoners are soldiers.

Dr. Frankl was a neurologist and psychiatrist as well as a holocaust survivor. He helped his fellow prisoners endure the harsh realities of camp life and improve their chances of survival by telling them to keep in touch with their spiritual life and to dwell in the spiritual domain—an area that the SS was unable to destroy.

> Everything can be taken from a man but the last of human freedoms, the right to choose one's attitude in any given set of circumstances, the right to choose one's own way (Dr. Viktor E. Frankl, 1905–1997).

When a person makes the choice to calmly manage a storm, to get up out of the ruins and rebuild, not only does that person become an inspiration to others, but he or she can draw personal inspiration from the memory of what he or she can do.

Any fact facing us is not as important as our attitude toward it, for that determines our success or failures (Norman Vincent Peale, 1898–1993).

We don't always have control over what comes our way, but we do control how we respond. There is a side to human nature that is wont to blow out of proportion the magnitude of the turmoil that comes its way, often calling a mild storm a hurricane and thus exaggerating its power. We can reduce the anguish we feel when we brace for life's storms by checking and asking ourselves what size we perceive this emotional turmoil to be. It is to our benefit to check our apprehension of what we are about to face and approach it with level-headedness, asking ourselves is this storm really a category five or just a cool breeze?

When stormy winds do pick up, I like to regain my composure with reassuring sayings, like, "All is well; just another cool breeze, with maybe a few strong gusts that I am sure I can handle." And I balance this with the secure thought that an SOS is always an option if the turmoil increases to a category five storm.

Sometimes it may take our inner strength and courage
to put into effect calm and positive attitudes,
but the results can be more far-reaching
than we ever thought possible.

Calm & Peace

2

~~~

~~~~

Knowledge and Wisdom

The essence of man

The current global average life expectancy for a human is 64.3 years.[1] Although death may mean the end of our physical body, most of mankind believes in an afterlife—that we will continue for eternity in one form or another. The thought of being around for longer than we can comprehend arouses most people's interest. Hence, in societies and religions, there is a diverse range of beliefs, with particular interest given to our soul and spirit.

---

[1] geography.about.com/od/populationgeography/a/lifeexpectancy.htm.

Like many others, I believe that God created us in his image, and that God offers a way for us to live with Him forever in heaven. Although I have this hope, and from the descriptions I have read of heaven, something amazing to look forward to, it is equally important to me that I make the most of the intricate mix that makes up who I am right here and now, given the storms and battles that will undoubtedly come my way.

The following divinely inspired proverbs recommend knowledge, understanding, wisdom, and a calm spirit as beneficial for everyday living.

> The proverb "A man's spirit will sustain him in sickness"[ii] is similar to the saying "Keep your spirits up." Two more proverbs declare, "He who gets wisdom loves his own soul; he who cherishes understanding prospers"[iii] and "He who has knowledge spares his words, and a man of understanding is of a calm spirit"[iv].

I will be honest, it never ceases to amaze me how quickly my internal dialogue can whip up a storm of negativity over an issue and adversely affect my emotions. Desiring to keep my emotions working for me not against me, I am learning to pay close attention to my internal conversations. I will admit there are times I need to give myself firm encouragement to forgo spirit-destroying dialogue and implement the above profound advice, advice that has proven worthy to be handed down from generation to generation.

The older I become, the more I am inspired to seek the knowledge that will help me overcome one of life's more intricate challenges - that of developing a calm spirit that will enrich my life and the lives of those around me.

Information overload

Wisdom and knowledge have been shared since the beginning of time. In the Bible, the well-known eviction of mankind from the Garden of Eden records an increase in man's knowledge due to Adam and Eve not heeding the following warning from God: "But you must not eat from the tree of the knowledge of good and evil, for when you eat of it you will surely die"[v]. We know that they did not physically die at this point, but they did receive the knowledge of good and evil: "Then the serpent said to the woman, 'You will not surely die. For God knows that in the day you eat of it your eyes will be opened and you will be like God, knowing good and evil'"[vi]. What an enticement - to be like God and to gain more knowledge. It may have sounded appealing to acquire this knowledge, but it would not surprise me if this newfound information came as a shock to Adam and Eve.

The death announced here by God and understood by theologians is the death of a spiritual connection to God. The Bible does explain that there is a way to reconnect with God spiritually. He also promises that those who reunite with Him will be given a helper to navigate them through the information overload of both good and evil: "But the Counselor, the Holy Spirit, whom the Father will send in my name, will teach you all things"[vii].

Since its creation, the human race has had the ability and freedom to make decisions. And the effects of man's decisions have been both peaceful and devastating. The New Testament suggests that Satan is still present today, offering advice and trying to influence people's decisions, just as he did with Adam and Eve: "That ancient serpent called the devil or Satan who leads the whole world astray"[viii]. However, Paul believes that we can protect ourselves with God's armor, as noted in his letter to the Ephesians: "Put on the full armor of God so that you can take your stand against the devils schemes"[ix]. More on Paul's description of God's armor can be found in Ephesians 6:10–18.

The value of wisdom

According to the Bible, around 1025 BC, a shepherd boy and direct descendent of Abraham, David, became a legend for slaying Goliath. Goliath was a giant of a man who was easily twice the size and strength of David. However, this young shepherd boy went on to become a great warrior for King Saul. As David's popularity grew, so did Saul's jealousy, eventually turning to hatred. Much is written concerning David's relationship with God amid his conflicts with Saul. After Saul's death, David is selected to ascend to his throne as the king of the Israelites. As king, he makes some foolish choices, but he also achieves some great successes. His writings in the Psalms offer encouragement to the reader, as the writings reflect both his struggles and his answers for calm amid the storms in his life.

> When I said, "My foot is slipping," your love O LORD, supported me. When anxiety was great within me, your consolation brought joy to my soul (King David).[x]

I appreciate David and the many others like him for their open and honest testimonies of how God's love helped them with their struggles and mistakes. I find it very encouraging to know that I am not the only person on this planet challenged by the knowledge of good and evil; I am not the only person seeking wisdom from God to help me make decisions that produce peace rather than turmoil.

After David's death, his son Solomon becomes the king. One night, God appears to King Solomon in a dream and says, "Solomon, ask for anything you want and I will give it to you." Solomon answers, "Give me the knowledge I'll need to be the king of this great nation of yours." God replies, "Solomon; you could have asked Me to make you rich or famous or to let you live a long time. Or you could have asked for your enemies to be destroyed. Instead, you asked for wisdom and knowledge to rule my people. So I will make you wise and intelligent. But I will also make you richer and more famous than any king before or after you"[xi].

Hearing of King Solomon's fame, the Queen of Sheba travels to Jerusalem to test his wisdom with difficult questions, of which he has no difficulty answering. Then, casting her eyes over his wealth, she responds, "Your wisdom and prosperity exceed the fame of which I heard. Happy are your men and happy are these, your servants, who stand continually before you and hear your wisdom!"[xii]

As a general rule, knowledge covers any and all information, and wisdom is the wise use of knowledge. We develop our wisdom using both ancient and modern knowledge. But ultimately

The real value in wisdom
comes in the decision to use it.

3

~~~

~~~~

Detect
And Treat

Detecting brewing negativity

Whenever a new strain of virus appears in society today, scientists identify it, create an antibiotic to treat it, and develop a vaccine to prevent it. Like scientists, we can detect any brewing negativity that contaminates our calm and peace, and treat it as they do a virus. We can discover our own antidotes to treat the negativity. As mentioned in Chapter 1, Libby Lenton kept a quote locked in her memory as her antidote against the external pressures that threatened negativity.

Like a virus, negativity can be contagious and can easily spread throughout the world. History has proven that a vaccine or antidote that is shared and dispensed throughout the world can make a fundamental difference. The World Health Organization declared that smallpox was eradicated in 1980 after a worldwide global vaccine campaign.[2] Smallpox was one of the world's most devastating diseases, originating 3,000 years ago and killing millions at a time. Nowadays, even our computers need protection from viruses. Thankfully, software companies have developed programs that quickly recognize and protect our computers from viruses and pop-ups. When negativity "pops up" in our own thinking, do we recognize it instantly? Would our calm and peace be enhanced if we were alert and prepared with an antidote to respond instantly to any negativity?

Hidden negativity can often reveal itself in one or all of the following niggles or thoughts: our work or school feels like a drag; our partner or family does not seem up to standard; our health is threatening to deteriorate;

---

[2] who.int/mediacentre/factsheets/smallpox/en/.

and finally—the big one on our list—will our pay or superannuation ever be enough? Do any of these, sound familiar?

Thankfully, little niggles do not necessarily draw the average person down into a black hole; they are comparable to the rumbling sounds of an approaching storm, just as gathering dark clouds precede a storm, even though one does not always read the signs. We tend not to fully identify the detrimental effects that regular negative thinking has until they appear in other forms such as losing our passion for life, becoming irritated far too easily, developing stress-related disorders including insomnia and high blood pressure, which can lead to a heart attack, or comfort eating that can result in obesity and diabetes.

Have you ever dipped into the never-ending list of "if only"? "If only I had the job of my dreams, a huge bank account, better health... If only my partner/family would change..." And my personal favorite, "If only I could win the lottery, then everything would be different." Sadly, we include a sense of failure whenever we use the words "if only." Failure also rears its ugly head when we use phrases such as "How did I end up here?" Or "How come I haven't got...?" A sense of failure merely adds weight to the original issues and drags us down even further.

But do not let such thoughts worry you—you are not alone. Some of us add even more weight to our issues by entering into *the blame game*, thinking over our history, trying to figure out whether we can blame someone else for our own predicament. Then we jump into our future and mess that up as well, adding fearful thoughts like "If things haven't improved by now, they probably never will!" Believing that there is no chance for change increases the likelihood of our stagnating and remaining in our current situation. "Thank goodness we have the weekends," you might say, or "I'll be happy when..." But is projecting our happiness into a hypothetical future the answer? Can this really beat a consistent calm inner peace?

Some feel life is like an endless marathon
and perceive death as the finish line;
while others seek out the good in life's journey
and anticipate death as a new beginning.

One simple antidote to negative thinking is to refocus on something good.

Good thoughts and actions bring a smile,
and a smile becomes contagious.

We have a moment to choose

Our attitudes do influence our life and the lives of others; therefore, attitudes are worthy of reflection. At times, all that is standing between the right attitude and us is a split second decision.

Between stimulus and response there is a space. In that space is our power to choose our response. In our response lie our growth and our freedom (Dr. Viktor E. Frankl, 1905–1997).

One part of any sporting competitor's training program involves studying the opponent's strategies in order to recognize and repel his or her advances, thereby seeking to obtain or maintain victory over the opponent. Similarly, we can also benefit from recognizing negative thoughts quickly in order to possibly repel them the second they invade.

The meaning of the word "antidote" is "a remedy to counteract the effects of poison"; the free dictionary includes an example of emotional poison: "Hallie's family life is laced with the poison of self-hatred, a poison that Sam has antidoted with love and understanding" (Christopher Swan). [3]

I personally include forgiveness high in my list of antidotes to counteract emotional poison. Emotional poison affects everyone and my experience has shown that the world has a wide range of antidotes for us to discover and share. This has really inspired me, and I hope to set up a website where others can share their calm and peace restoring antidotes; antidotes to help

---

[3] thefreedictionary.com/antidote.

against the viral negativity that dominates society. This website address will be calmandpeace.com.

The blame game

The blame game seems to come easily to most people, and this can include blaming others as well as ourselves for any problems that we face. It is widely taught that those seeking a new outlook on life need to take a good hard look in the mirror, stop playing the blame game, quit "stinking thinking,"[4] and start to improve how they process their thoughts.

I wanted to walk away from the mirror when I saw my hidden negativity producing time-wasting thinking. My thoughts had been content with the idea that all of my problems were the result of the people around me not being perfect as I was (ha ha)! So, I had to conjure some inner strength to stop playing the blame game.

The reality is that the blame game provides us with excuses that lead to a feeling of hopelessness; for example, "It is their fault, and I can't do a thing about it."

---

[4] "Stinking thinking": thoughts that are so unhelpful, they stink.

Blaming ourselves or others, can be a form of giving up and giving away control.

Blame should only ever be a visitor—not a dweller. It is true that we may need to discover what or who the cause of a problem is, but it is how we respond at the point of discovery that determines whether we then move forward or backward. More often than not, forgiveness is the key to moving forward. Sadly, when it comes to forgiveness, no one really feels like doing it, much in the same way that no one feels like taking out the garbage, which just gets heavier and smellier the longer it sits!

The baggage of un-forgiveness weighs down the eagle, releasing the baggage, he soars to new heights.

To forgive is to set a prisoner free and discover the prisoner was you (Lewis B. Smedes).[5]

Some people use alcohol or drugs to find a temporary release from troubling issues, but eventually, this only

---

[5] thinkexist.com/quotes/Lewis_B._Smedes/.

adds to their suffering. It can take years for some to work out whom to forgive, but thankfully, many do come to the realization of forgiveness, which sets them free. I know that I need to work on paying very close attention so that I don't let little issues stir up into storms that can drench me, and others as well. Little grudges still need forgiveness.

> *In sport, we work out for personal bests.*
> *In life, we work it out for personal peace.*
> *For personal bests in personal peace,*
> *We need to work on working it out.*

One of the greatest moments in anybody's developing experience is when he no longer tries to hide from himself, but determines to get acquainted with himself as he really is (Norman Vincent Peale, 1898–1993).

Often, I have expected instant change and an automatic desire to improve, both from myself and from those around me. Finally, I realized that we need to accept that people are just people, and they are capable of good and not so good—and this includes me!

Jerry Waxler wrote a very good thesis on blame that can be found on the Internet.[6] I particularly liked the following section: "Since our problems are caused by other people, we hope they'll be solved by other people. We passively wait for a rescuer."

I believe that I have done this. In hindsight, I also believe that on some occasions when I have shared my problems with more than one person, I was probably looking for a rescuer. With this wonderful revelation and given that waiting for a rescuer or for others to change or even to say that they are sorry just leaves me in a waiting room, I had a good laugh at myself and wondered if that is really where I want to be. I made a resolution to unlock these waiting room doors with the key of forgiveness, and to develop for myself a vibrant new *living* room.

---

[6] mental-health-survival-guide.com/blame.htm.

I had to go through an interesting workout to forgive both others and myself for the disappointments and grudges that I had held onto, and I wrote the following prayer to use at the time, which I still find helpful today.

Lord, help me let go of
blaming and judgmental thoughts.
Lord, grant me the strength to stand for what is right
and even greater strength to show tolerance,
love, understanding, and forgiveness
to those who have wronged me,
including myself.

Although this may sound easy, tolerance and forgiveness were then and continue to be quite a workout. However, I am seeing the rewards they bring, and these are inspiring me to persevere. Moving forward can involve taking a stance or instigating some changes. I was glad to exchange the time that I spent blaming people with time better spent seeking a peaceful solution. I could then take the next step and build up my courage and ability to implement changes.

It was incredibly liberating, finally, to get out of the blame spiral and become a solution seeker.

"The More we sweat in Peace the less we bleed in war (Vijaya Lakshmi Pandit, 1900–1990)."[7] Vijava Lakshmi Pandit was a female Indian diplomat who led India's first goodwill mission to China.

---

[7] quotegarden.com/peace.html.

4

~~~

~~~~

Viruses
And Antidotes

The subtle forms of evil

"For where you have envy and selfish ambition, there you find disorder and every evil practice."[xiii]

The word "evil" often pertains to Satan and his minions. "Evil" also describes the dark consequences of hate, and immoral or cruel actions or thoughts; "good," in contrast, is virtuous and caring. Most people do not like to think that they partake in evil, but evil has a way of sneaking up on us. We have evidence of this in the

43

Bible, dating back around 6,000 years, in the account of Cain allowing his feelings of jealousy over an offering to develop into a rage that leads him to kill his brother, Abel, even though the Lord had alerted him of the danger of envy.

> Then the Lord said to Cain, "Why are you angry? Why is your face downcast? If you do what is right, will you not be accepted? But if you do not do what is right, sin is crouching at your door; it desires to have you, but you must master it!"[xiv]

The above advice has been handed down and shared in a variety of ways. One version between friends or family could sound like this: "What's up with you, you need to change your attitude, you can do better, that sort of thinking will lead you astray, get a grip before you do something you regret." The tale of two wolves handed down as Cherokee wisdom notes our battle with the knowledge of good and evil, and it includes a very simple antidote that is easy to remember.

~ Two Wolves ~

One evening, an old Cherokee told his grandson
about a battle that goes on inside people.
He said, "My son, the battle is between
two wolves inside us all.
One is Evil—it is anger, envy, jealousy, sorrow,
regret, greed, arrogance, self-pity, guilt, resentment,
inferiority, lies, false pride, superiority, and ego.
The other is good—it is joy, peace, love, hope,
serenity, humility, kindness, benevolence, empathy,
generosity, truth, compassion, and faith."
The grandson thought for a moment
and then asked; "Which wolf wins?"
The old Cherokee simply replied,
"The one you feed."

God encourages us to "depart from evil and do good;
seek peace and pursue it"[xv].

Stillness, serenity, and quietness, which are forms of calm, relate well to the more commonly known three-step process: stop, look, and listen!

Stop – virus alert!

Stop = Stillness.

The first step is to recognize more quickly when we shift to negative thinking, the feeling of being downcast, or the brewing of a storm so that we can make an immediate stop. In our fast-paced society, no one really wants to stop; but remember, it is far better to stop and delete a virus than to let it ruin the whole computer. Continuing to think negatively in the direction of evil is like the captain of a ship heading straight for a storm without considering his options. The sayings "count to ten" and "take a deep breath" have been around for years and are useful, but the saying "hold on; what is really going on here?" includes a complete stop and begins the next step in the process: looking.

Recognize and stop!
Stop and recognize!

Listen to your internal dialogue

Look = Serenity.

We need to look into what we are really thinking internally, as this is producing frustrated and disturbed feelings, and ask, "What has disturbed my calm right now? Is it envy, jealousy, hatred, blaming, or un-forgiveness? When did it start?" Sometimes, we may find that it started years ago and that something has happened to bring it up again. Was it an event or someone else's careless words? Is it something recurrent? This exercise is the equivalent of retracing your steps when you have lost something.

Look at whether you are trying to *justify* being disturbed with negative feelings. If we do not want to forgive or admit that we may have been in the wrong, we can begin to justify the disturbance (i.e., envy, hatred, etc.) that we feel, which can steer us away from seeking a peaceful resolution.

It is better to deal with our disturbances
before our disturbances deal with us!

Discover and implement antidotes

Listen = Quietness.

Listen as you replace any negative responses with positive words or affirmations. Remember, this is your first opportunity to reject the subtle advances of evil. Listen as you remind yourself that you are not alone; everyone gets tempted or faces tough decisions at some point in their life. Listen to encouraging words like "hang on," "be strong," "this challenge (storm) will pass," and "your strength will shine through." Replace evil thoughts with good thoughts and reinforce with positive statements of good outcomes.

Negatives stifle the air,
positives are the fresh breeze that offers relief.

In the New Testament, James writes the following:

Or take ships as an example. Although they are so large and are driven by strong winds, they are steered by a very small rudder wherever the pilot wants to go. Likewise the tongue is a small part of the body, but it makes great boasts. Consider what a great forest is set on fire by a small spark. The tongue also is a fire, a world of evil among the parts of the body. It corrupts the whole person, sets the whole course of his life on fire, and is itself set on fire by hell.[xvi]

Preventing unnecessary turmoil is about steering your ship, i.e., yourself, by controlling your tongue, as James so aptly put it, preferably toward calmer waters. When it comes to your options of what to say in the midst of a situation, your tongue will reveal your choice. If you hear yourself making a wrong choice, remember that the tongue is only "set on fire by hell," or ignited by the subtle forms of evil, for the length of time that we allow it to continue. We have the choice to stop and change what we are saying mid-sentence! We have the option to discover and take aboard wise sayings and thoughts that when imbedded in the mind, produce peace.

It is easier to put out a match than a forest fire,
so too
it is easier to extinguish evil thoughts as they spark.

Keep your eyes on the prize and your tongue steering you in the direction of calm and peace; the same goes for our internal dialogue.

"And goodness is the harvest that is produced from the seeds the peacemakers plant in peace"[xvii].

I have set out a few examples of unsettling virus-like thoughts and calmer thinking antidotes:

~ Viruses ~	~ Antidotes ~
Things will never change	All things are possible
(Sinking the ship with doubt)	*(Discover new lands)*
My life Sucks	My life is good and getting better
(Sailing into fog)	*(Sailing out of fog)*
I am sick of everything	Rediscover contentment
(Dropping Anchor)	*(Bring out the binoculars)*

I can't do anything	Let's see what I can do.
(Mutiny)	*(Finding courage)*
They are not worth it	God loves them
(Have them walk the Plank)	*(Drop them off at port)*
How come I don't have..?	Count your blessings
(All at sea without a Paddle)	*(Finding a sail)*
Speaking negatively	Speaking positively
(Firing the cannon)	*(Sharing Treasure)*
Fear	Fear Not
Why me?	Why not me?
Attack and destroy	Peace and Caring
Revenge	Forgive
I hate	I Love

How vast is man's choice of words!
How liberating are the right combinations!

More often than not, the private act of understanding, accepting, and forgiving something or someone, including ourselves plays a major role in reinstating our calm. Reinhold Niebuhr (1892–1971) put this well in the serenity prayer.

~ The Serenity Prayer ~

God grant me the serenity to accept the things I cannot change, courage to change the things I can, and wisdom to know the difference.

Importantly, acceptance does not mean that we desire or approve of what needs accepting. Acceptance and forgiveness are freeing actions (antidotes) against an undesired disturbance.

Like a sportsman, with practice I am finding it easier to steer my ship in the right direction using "stop, look, and listen," combined with forgiveness, love, wise sayings, and refocusing.

Have I mentioned laughter and singing? As the saying goes, laughter is the best medicine. I once heard of a school principal who set up a laugh committee that had the job of posting one-liners around the office. He received offerings such as "If your parents didn't have children, you won't either." And with a little research, I found "Consciousness: that annoying time between naps!" As we move along on the conveyer belt of time, one thing never changes: the right song can lift the spirits of one person or an entire audience.

A merry heart doeth good, like medicine.[xviii]

Calm & Peace

5

~~~

~~~~

Igniting a Calm Attitude

Speak in the affirmative (antidotes)

I remember learning a long time ago that one should take care in the phrasing of words for positives outcomes. Example: "Don't think of turmoil" can, in fact, leave us thinking of turmoil, whereas we have a better chance of thinking of calm with the positive phrasing, "think of calm." If this idea is combined with the theory that the last word you hear will be the one that you focus on, which would be better, "don't wriggle" or "sit still," when you are trying to calm a child? To calm a storm raging around the boat that he and others are in,

Jesus says, "Peace, be still!" Similarly, I have heard teenagers say, "It's all good," and inspirational writers teach, "All is well."

Double hit negatives

Have you heard the saying, "If you can't say anything nice, it is better to say nothing at all"? Well, I want to share with you an antidote that takes this saying to a different level. For every negative that you speak or think of, replace it with *two* positives. In theory, starting at ground level, one negative would take you down one, then two positives would take you back to ground level and one rung above. So, the more positives you embrace, the higher you will climb.

Up
Rethink
I can rebound
__ Ground Level __
Oops! sinking
Setback
Down

This presented an interesting challenge for me, so I monitored it closely. I noticed that in conversations about people, I felt more peaceful when I began adding a couple of positives after a negative would slip out.

Stoking up the right attitude

Mornings are an opportune time to recognize negative thoughts that need replacing, since negative thoughts or memories, especially traumatic memories, can flood in as we awaken. One of my less traumatic repeaters, and one you may recognize, is "I don't want to get out of bed; it is a work day." I now respond to this with "recognize the negative attitude in those words and give them a flick." I like to feel my frown lines soften as I replace negatives with positives.

I am learning to increase my awareness of precious moments in my day, like the prospector who learns to recognize precious gems in the rough. Nowadays the more I treasure in my everyday life and in the people around me, the more I enjoy a boost to my morale.

When life gives you a hundred reasons to cry; show life that you have a thousand reasons to smile (Author unknown).

The twenty-third Psalm is well-known and has offered help to millions of people, especially those dealing with a traumatic experience. I recently went through a serious family drama, so I printed off a copy of the twenty-third Psalm to read whenever I needed reassurance from God. In addition to finding the reassurance I was looking for, I noticed that these words read like a reassuring ladder, rising from one uplifting positive statement to another and another.

The Lord is my shepherd; I shall not be in want. He makes me lie down in green pastures, He leads me beside quiet waters, He restores my soul. He guides me in paths of righteousness for his name's sake. Even though I walk through the valley of death, I will fear no evil, for You are with me; Your rod and Your staff, they comfort me. You prepare a table before me in the presence of my enemies. You anoint my head with oil: my cup overflows. Surely goodness and love will follow me all the days of my life, and I will dwell in the house of the Lord forever. Twenty-third Psalm[xix]

I was listening to Terri Irwin from Australia Zoo in her first interview after the untimely death of her husband Steve, the Crocodile Hunter. She spoke about his great passion for life and how he would always wake up very early, excited to go and do something. As I listened, I reflected on how the enthusiastic and caring way in which Steve Irwin spoke about everything that captured the hearts of the millions who watched his shows. "I *love* animals, I *love* wildlife! Don't you just *love* the way they curl their little tails? I *love* what I do!" Steve used to say.

He had a passion, and he was not afraid to use the word "love." So, just how far did his focus on love and caring take him, and in reality, just how dangerous and exhausting was his work? Well, his passion took him far enough to wrestle with crocodiles and love them. Let's face it, most of our daily challenges are a bit like crocodiles, biting and snapping at us when we least expect it, and a focused attitude—one that allows a passion for calm, love, and caring to prevail—is part of successfully wrestling with them. Hunters bind the mouth of a crocodile to subdue it; this visual of the hunters pouncing and binding is one that I use when I notice that I need to restrain the negative words coming out of my mouth—words that may be harmful to me or to others.

If you take the time to listen closely, you will be shocked, or at least surprised, at how many negatives human beings accept as natural, and the degree to which we immerse or indulge ourselves in this type of thinking. If you find it difficult to exchange two positives for one negative about a person or a situation, then simply try to avoid the negative in the first place.

The way of life winds upward for the wise that he may turn away from the hell below[xx] (Proverb).

Changing attitudes

The words "love" and "hate" have a force of propulsion behind them. The former makes a smile; the latter brings a frown. I started to struggle with thoughts such as, "Oh boy I hate doing this," and "Man I hate the way they do that!"

When inner turmoil is ablaze by pointless hate
fight for your calm with buckets of love.

After purchasing a home, I was challenged by this type of storm brewing negativity. The previous owner had arranged for the beautiful terracotta-colored, ceramic tile pathway at the entry to be painted black. The quality of workmanship was shocking, and the paint was slippery and peeling. Needless to say, I became quite upset at the days of paint-stripping and hard work that loomed. "If only" crept into my thinking; "If only the previous owner had just left it alone." From this, I spiraled down to a level where I was telling myself, "I *hate* having to fix up bad work!"

When I recognized hate creeping into my thoughts; 'I asked myself, "How can I turn my negative attitude around?"' I began by censoring my words and thoughts, with the aim to delete the debilitating hate. More notably, I felt that this negative attitude was blocking my harmony with God. I decided to fire up a conversation with God and ask for His help to rekindle the loving thoughts within me. "Dear Lord, let me not waste another minute whining over the things over which I have or had no control." Note: Sometimes, other parties are at fault and need forgiveness, but mostly, it is our attitude that needs forgiveness.

After I prayed further, "Lord, forgive me for the thoughts and actions that were not loving, calm, or peaceful; Lord, help me change my negative attitude into a positive one," I experienced a release of the negativity that had consumed me. With some help, and my changed attitude, the job was completed smoothly. The lesson from this experience is that pointless hate will always take us down; forgiveness, love, and acceptance provide the elevator back up.

The meaning of things lies not in the things themselves, but in our attitude towards them (Antoine De Saint Exupery).

Monitor unruly thoughts, nurture a calm attitude

The expression "get over it!" can appear insulting if you do not think that you are in the wrong, but the truth is that half of us do not know how to get over it, whatever "it" may be. All we know is that we have a feeling or power inside us that we are not sure how to control.

Be careful how you think;
your life is shaped by your thoughts.[xxi]

"Getting over it" can merely involve a change of attitude. I practice attitude switches a lot; the most common occurrence is when no one helps with the dishes. I switch my thoughts from "I hate doing dishes" to "I love a clean kitchen." However, I do have to ask myself if I really wanted their help, or if it was my own attitude toward work that brought negativity into the situation. On the other hand, I ask if it was my own fear that prevented me from asking for help, that is, if I was afraid of an awful response. Times have changed and lifestyles are different; modern families are involved in a lot of extra activities. Did I need to review the former designated roles designating who should be doing what?

What works in one home may not work in another. If some people are not pulling their weight, we must either forgive them or negotiate with them, and it requires strength to do either one. There may be times when we need to seek professional help, and I won't argue that the fees for this often seem outrageous, but so is the pain of mental anguish, divorce, or a poor relationship with our children. We have all learned the value of having a hole fixed in our tooth before it becomes more painful, deteriorates with decay, and falls out. We are worth much more than a tooth, as are our relationships. There is value in spending the necessary amount of time and money early on to repair any decay that is forming in either our minds or in our relationships.

Stand up to your obstacles and do something about them. You will find that they haven't half the strength you think they have! (Norman Vincent Peale, 1898–1993).

Daily, we are faced with various kinds of letdowns and mishaps. I started the process of dealing with these events calmly by renaming them as "situations." For example, I changed the old saying, "I am having a bad day," to, "I have a few situations to attend to/deal with." When things go wrong, I say to myself, "Well, that's an interesting event, but I know that I can handle it." When I feel like I have failed, I turn this around by saying, "Now, there's an experience for you," or, "I know a good antidote for this." Albert Einstein (1879–1955) put this excellently: "A person, who never made a mistake, never tried anything new." And I heard this little gem recently - they wouldn't put an eraser on the end of a pencil if people didn't need it.

I have also learned to ask for time to think when a situation or request has caught me off-guard; for example, in a work situation and even with my teenagers, I will say, "This will take some thinking over, so I'll need to get back to you on this."

It is a challenge when we receive an unexpected blow from someone, but now my response is, "Wow, I didn't see that one coming." I know that I should not let an unwarranted sting in other people's words affect me, and so I choose to leave their words with them, brushing their impact off with the same enthusiasm that I would brush from my body mites or ticks, which can burrow in and get under my skin. Harsh words can leave a surface sting in your mind, like a mosquito bite on your skin, and just as scratching slows the healing process of a bite, so repeatedly reliving what people say will slow our healing from a verbal attack. We may need to give the conversation some reflection and question seriously whether we unwittingly provoked them, or consider that they might be going through a tough time. I know that these activities give me an opportunity to remedy my response and to decide whether the need for forgiveness or understanding lies with me or with them. Mankind has learned to enjoy nature and to manage mosquito bites in a number of ways; in the same way, it is up to us to learn how to manage conversations with the people around us. On the positive side, most experiences enhance our future by making us a little wiser.

> You know that forgiveness has begun when you recall those who hurt you and you feel the power to wish them well (Lewis B. Smedes).[8]

---

[8] thinkexist.com/quotes/Lewis_B._Smedes/.

Calm & Peace

6

~~~

~~~~

Peaceful Responses

Fair and Unfair

What is fair about one person dying of starvation while another dies of obesity? Life itself is unfair, and we see examples of this all around us. The age-old statement, "How come they have… and I don't? It's so unfair," echoes from the mouths of the very young to the very old. God responds to this sentiment in the last of the Ten Commandments: "You shall not covet"[xxii]. In saying this, I think He simply means that the reason why we should not covet is because coveters can experience envy, despair, and frustration.

What is considered fair and unfair is hotly debated within most families, parliaments, and by almost anyone who has a voice. Those who blame God for not taking control over every situation would cry out for the freedom that they lost if he did take control. God encourages (rather than controls) us to love, respect, and choose wisely.

From a very young age, we consider it unfair for someone to cut in. This ruffles most of us, firstly, with the frustration of wasting more time in the line; secondly, with the dilemma of whether we should say something; and thirdly, with the challenge not to judge the person who cut in (e.g., "That's right—your type always cuts in!"). There is no harm in politely saying, "Do you realize that is not the end of the line?" I now convert these experiences into an opportunity to test out my stress antidotes and to reflect on how long it took me this time to forgive and to start smiling.

Another form of unfairness concerns whining and complaining, often about something that has nothing to do with me whatsoever; this can come from family or co-workers. I have taught myself to keep my responses short, learning from a story in Mark 4:37–41: "When the disciples woke Jesus because of a great windstorm that arose and the waves were beating into the boat as he slept, they did so with a complaint. 'Teacher, do you not care that we are perishing?' Jesus then spoke to the storm. 'Peace, be still!'" This is a good example of Jesus using short and positive words to calm both the storm and his disciples. When my own mind or someone else's presents a storm of negativity, I like to respond using the saying, "I am sure there is a calm solution here!" A friend shared with me that his response to lazy teenagers who should fix their own problem is, "I am not sure if your problem needs to become my problem—I am sure you can work this one out."

In life, there are extreme levels of unfair experiences for innocent victims, for example, a child dying as the result of a hit and run by a drunk driver. It is not uncommon for people in these situations, or even less extreme ones, to use the word "unforgivable" or phrases such as "it is just too hard to forgive" or "I'll never forgive."

However, we can be encouraged by the testimonies of people who have found the strength to forgive. Some have refocused their lives and set up foundations and educational programs as a result of what they have been through. One good example is TKF—Tariq-Khamisa Foundation - tkf.org, a foundation set up in October 1995 by Azim Khamisa, who decided to choose forgiveness over the usual retribution when his 21-year-old son Tariq Khamisa, who was delivering pizza, was murdered for the pizza money by 14-year-old Tony Hicks, who was acting under orders from his 18-year-old gang leader. Instead of focusing on his loss, Azim saw the loss of two American sons—one forever, and one to the state prison system. He said, "Change is urgently needed in a society where children kill children." Azim now spends his time with Ples Felix, the guardian and grandfather of Tony Hicks (Tony is now serving 25 years in prison). The two have joined forces to speak to tens of thousands of school children about the "power of forgiveness" to break the cycle of violence through the TKF Violence Impact Forum program.

An acquaintance of mine suffered from pain in her left leg from the age of 17, when a driver running a red light hit the bike that she and her partner were riding. The accident happened in Germany, in a town where it was customary for the police to bring the offender to the hospital to see the victim, giving the offender a chance to say sorry. I will never forget her words: "As I lay there in pain, I was shocked when he not only refused to say sorry but he walked up and spat at me." She went on to say that she only felt sorry for him, as she knew that he had rejected an opportunity to find peace—the peace she was able to find in forgiveness. In a world where this is not an isolated case, we can realize that peace is found in forgiveness, and it is not reliant on the offender's apology.

Forgiveness is a funny thing; it warms the heart and cools the sting (William Arthur Ward, 1921–1994).[9]

---

[9] thinkexist.com/quotations/forgiveness/.

Corrie Ten Boom was a Dutch Christian imprisoned by the Nazis for hiding Jews during World War II. She barely survived the horrors of the Holocaust in Ravensbrueck, and she became famous for her book *The Hiding Place*. She embarked on speaking engagements to talk to thousands of people, sharing her faith and the importance of forgiveness, as taught by Jesus Christ himself. At the end of a meeting one night, a man confronted her and asked if he could receive the forgiveness of Christ of which she had spoken. She recognized him as a guard from Ravensbrueck. She instantly felt all of the hatred and pain for those years of persecution. She silently prayed for God to give her the strength to forgive the man. She soon felt a sensation begin in her heart and flow through her hand as it touched his (Corrie Ten Boom, *The Hiding Place*, Hodder and Stoughton, 1971). Corrie believed that "God will give us the love to be able to forgive our enemies."[10]

When one heart forgives,
two hearts rejoice.

---

[10] corrietenboom.com/history.htm.

The calm and confidence of a King

When Jesus walked the earth as a man and the King of the Jews approximately 2,000 years ago, his mission was to bring peace to all mankind. This mission included personal suffering, which he foretells in the following statement to his disciples: "I must go to Jerusalem. There the nations' leaders, the chief priests, and the teachers of the Law of Moses will make me suffer terribly. I will be killed, but three days later I will rise to life"[xxiii].

Wanting to connect with all of mankind regardless of social status or culture, Jesus shows His calm willingness and openness to speak to anyone, even though he suffers reprisals for doing so. "And they shall call His name Immanuel, which is translated 'God with us.'"[xxiv] He does not choose the easy path of attracting loyalty as a wealthy, majestic King, or through fame and the admiration of good looks. "He had no beauty or majesty to attract us to him, nothing in his appearance that we should desire him."[xxv] Jesus refuses the devil's offer of superhero displays such as jumping off the temple and having God's angels catch him. "'If you are the Son of God,' he [the devil] said, 'throw yourself down. For it is written: He will command his angels concerning you, and they will lift you up in their hands.'"[xxvi] Furthermore, Jesus refuses the Pharisees' request for signs, miracles, and wonders: "The Pharisees came and began to question Jesus. To test him, they asked him for a sign from heaven. He sighed deeply and said, 'Why does this generation ask for a miraculous sign? I tell you the truth, no sign will be given it'"[xxvii]. Although he is known to perform many miracles, he does not do this as a tool to gain approval.

Jesus explains why He is prepared to allow himself to be arrested when Peter draws his sword and cuts off the ear of a soldier who is arresting Jesus. He says, "Do you think I cannot call on my Father, and He will at once put at my disposal more than twelve legions of angels? But how then would the Scriptures be fulfilled that say it must happen in this way?"[xxviii] He remains calm when the chief priests falsely accuse him: "And the Chief Priests accused Him of many things, but He answered nothing; then Pilate asked Him again saying, 'Do you answer nothing? See how many things they testify against You!' But Jesus answered nothing, so that Pilate marveled"[xxix].

Jesus forewarns the disciples that He is going to allow His own death on the cross: "Therefore My Father loves Me, because I lay My life that I may take it again. No one takes it from Me, but I lay it down Myself. I have power to lay it down, and I have power to take it again. This command I have received from My Father"[xxx]. We also know that it is His choice to atone for the sins of the people: "For even the Son of Man did not come to be served, but to serve, and to give His life a ransom for many"[xxxi]. Christians acknowledge that there is a price to be paid for sin and are thankful to Jesus for paying their sin debt, thus giving them the opportunity to reunite with God both now and eternally. There is no doubt in my mind that it required real purpose to be who He was and to endure such atrocities, and to choose to remain calm amidst the storm of betrayal and arrest.

I find it stirring that He did this with human limitations. Jesus shared an incredible example of forgiveness in the final minutes of His life when, as he hung in agony on the cross, he said, "Father, forgive them, for they do not know what they are doing"[xxxii].

7

~~~

~~~~

Turning
Fear Around

Love drives out fear

Fear is pain arising from the anticipated evil.
He who overcomes his fears will truly be free.
(Aristotle, 384 BC–322 BC).

A strangler fig or a parasite attaches itself to and engulfs a host, sometimes ultimately killing the host. Like a strangler fig or a parasite, fearful thoughts also attach themselves to and engulf our thoughts about whatever it is we are doing. The mind can only think about one thing at a time, but we often dart back and forth between multiple subjects. Fear-related thoughts can multiply and create a storm of fear in our minds; this may then compromise or divert our focus. There is no harm in being aware of the dangers that surround us, or that may affect an issue; but in order for us to give our scrupulous attention to what we are doing or thinking about, it is helpful to recognize and then settle stormy fear into calm awareness or to change from being alarmed to being alert.

"There is no fear in love, but perfect love drives out fear."[xxxiii] Love—both our emotional love and God's perfect love—can help to drive out fear. One example that I have found helpful is when I am driving on the highway or around town and a truck comes alongside me, I think to myself, "Sure, I need to be aware of the truck, but let's just keep it to awareness"; I keep my focus on my driving and cast out fear by saying, "I love an opportunity to become more confident around trucks; I love the benefit that trucks are to society; I love getting safely past a truck."

From a very young age, we begin to recognize the good feeling of love when it surrounds us, and the empty feeling when it doesn't. We may fear losing, missing out on, or being hurt by love. We should prevent fear from ever engulfing love, as love is the very thing that we need to drive out fear. It is vitally important to protect our ability to both give out and receive love, because it is in giving that we will receive, and it is in receiving that we will discover that love can be found in places and come from hearts that we never expected. I would like to encourage everyone to seek the love and joy that God freely offers; I am discovering that He has plenty to give.

The word "love" has various meanings, and countless books have been written about love, but I find the following description both clear and easy to remember:

> Love is kind and patient, never jealous, boastful, proud, or rude. Love isn't selfish or quick tempered. It doesn't keep a record of the wrongs that others do. Love rejoices in the truth, but not evil. [xxxiv]

Fearful feelings can sprout from envy or jealousy. Firstly, to clarify the positive side of envy, we can identify the things that we desire and be inspired to work toward acquiring them. Jealousy may also be converted into a calm protectiveness of that which is ours, most noticeably our careers or relationships. However, the fear that is connected to envy involves the fear of missing out, the discontentment and resentfulness that is aroused by another's success or possessions, even going as far as to desire that others lack as well; while for jealousy, it is the fear of losing someone's love or a job or a competition that induces anger and unhappiness during an unjustified rivalry.

Peace of mind makes the body healthy,
but jealousy is like cancer.[xxxv]

When I researched "dealing with envy or jealousy," I found that various professionals suggest that we deal with our insecurities and fears of rejection or lack, count our blessings and then count them again, work on and enjoy our abilities, develop our confidence, and be very reassuring of our self-worth.

It is better to overcome fear,
than to be overcome by fear.

My husband and I had our construction business sued as a result of an injury that occurred to a supplier's employee on one of our job sites. We were insured, and our insurance company granted the payout, but it took seven years to settle the case. Throughout that period, I feared that the insurance company might look for a loophole and declare that they would no longer cover us, in which case, we would lose everything and be paying off the settlement for the rest of our lives. The day that we received the summons was the worst, but I was comforted that day when I opened my Bible randomly and read this about God:

> There is no one like the God of Jeshurun, Who rides on the heavens to help you, and on the clouds in His majesty. The eternal God is your refuge, and underneath are the everlasting arms; He will drive out your enemy before you, saying, "Destroy Him!" [xxxvi]

I wrote this out and recite it to this day whenever my emotional enemies, those horrible parasites such as hatred, envy, and fear, threaten my peace.

While driving past a church early one morning, I read on their sign that the limits we put on God are not His true limits. I reassure myself of this when I need to build up my courage, asking myself, "Is God with me or not? Yes! Is God afraid? No! Then why should I be?" Fear can rob us of peace in all areas of our lives. Worry greatly depletes energy, which is a good reason to stay calm and rested so that we can be full of energy if we are needed in an emergency. When the storms that cause worry surround us, there is a calming antidote in Proverb 12:25: "Worry weighs a person down; an encouraging word lifts a person up."

> The more confidence you have in yourself and your ability to persevere, the better able you'll be to take a stressful situation in stride. (helpguide.org)

One day, I heard a true story on the radio that went something like this: A nurse in a hospital ward for dying children recalled the story of a five-year-old boy who was dying of lung cancer. She mentioned that this is a scary and painful way to die. During the day, the little boy kept telling her that he could hear bells ringing. That night, the nurse came into the room to see the boy's mother cradling him in her arms, and again, he was saying that he could hear bells ringing. The nurse tried to reassure the mother that the medication might be affecting him. But the mother replied, "I told my son, when the pain gets bad, look towards the corner of the ceiling and listen for the bells of heaven, as they will ring when someone is entering heaven."

The boy's mother gave him something positive to focus on—a diversion from the pain and any fear that he may have had of dying. For most of us, the fear of pain alone is bad enough, and we can benefit by remembering to restore our calm through focusing on a good element amid the bad ones.

I once told some friends that I feared for my future and those of my children unless the values of the world changed. One of them handed me a book with the core theme "change me." I remember thinking, "Why are you giving me this book?" But I understood by the second chapter that fear would not change anything; only our example will. I became more determined to work on my own values and cheerfulness, as my future and those of my children can be influenced by me. As for changing the world, I believe that a living example speaks louder than any poster.

Cheerfulness brightens lives,
like an oasis brings life to a desert.

Fear that our contribution is not good enough and fails to meet others' expectations can affect our courage to proceed. I wonder how many times fear has stifled a dream?

It is better to live rich than to die rich! (Samuel Johnson, 1709–1784).

8

~~~

~~~~

Empowered By Connection

Be taught by the best

I know that I am not perfect—I am human, after all. But I am extremely thankful that I have the choice and freedom to forgive and forget my mistakes, and not play the blame game. With the Lord as my coach, I know that I can learn how to cope and soar in all circumstances. "Those who hope in the Lord will renew their strength. They will soar on wings like eagles; they will run and not grow weary, they will walk and not be faint."[xxxvii] "For the eyes of the Lord range throughout the earth to strengthen those whose hearts are fully committed to Him."[xxxviii] "So do not fear, for I am with you; do not be dismayed, for I am your God. I will strengthen you and help you; I will uphold you with my righteous right hand."[xxxix]

If you have not yet made a reconnection with God, I urge you to do so. Not only will you enjoy the promise of your soul and spirit being united with God for eternity, "For God so loved the world that He gave His one and only son, that whoever believes in Him shall not perish but have eternal life"[xl]; you will also receive the benefits of a relationship with the Trinity (God, Jesus, and the Holy Spirit), having them as your coach to maintain the calm and confidence of a king in your daily life now! Jesus said, "But the Helper, the Holy Spirit, whom the Father will send in My name, He will teach you all things, and bring to your remembrance all things that I said to you. Peace I leave with you, My peace I give to you; not as the world gives do I give to you. Let not your heart be troubled, neither let it be afraid"[xli].

When Jesus died and rose to life again, He won a decisive victory for mankind over the devil's schemes, including the scheme to inflict a fear of death. "Since the children have flesh and blood, He(Jesus) too shared in their humanity so that by His death He might destroy him who holds the power of death – that is, the devil, and free those who all their lives were held in slavery by their fear of death. For surely it is not angels He helps, but Abraham's descendants. For this reason He had to be made like His brothers in every way, in order that He might become a merciful and faithful high priest in service to God, and that He might make atonement for the sins of the people. Because He Himself suffered when He was tempted, He is able to help those who are being tempted"[xlii].

Christians today and throughout history have attested to the relief and joy they feel when they put their faith in Jesus Christ. "That if you confess with your mouth the Lord Jesus and believe with your heart that God has raised Him from the dead, you will be saved."[xliii] Jesus provides more than one example in Luke 15 of the relief and joy expressed in heaven when someone repents and returns to God.

An expression of faith can be very simple, similar to the following, or it can be a personal outpouring spoken from the heart.

Thank you, Lord Jesus, for dying for any sin that I have been involved with, both knowingly and unknowingly. I believe that God raised you from the dead in a victorious battle for those desiring eternal peace.
I pray for the Holy Spirit to come into my heart and be my Helper.

Now, hope does not disappoint, because the love of God has been poured out in our hearts by the Holy Spirit who was given to us. [xliv]

Those who have returned to God the Father, Jesus, and the Holy Spirit can also be empowered with the calm and confidence that exist in the Trinity.

9

~~~

~~~~

Regaining Composure

A popular prayer

A few years ago, my husband, son, and I went driving around to have a look at a flash flood that had occurred after a heavy deluge in our area. The rain had stopped, and like everyone else who was out surveying the damage, we realized that this was like no other flash flood we had ever seen before. The water from upstream was still arriving. When we turned to go back the way we had come, there was water covering the road. As cars were still making it through, we decided to go for it. It turned out that ours was the very last vehicle to go through this water. About halfway through the flooded roadway, I felt the car rise momentarily. As I looked out the window, I could not believe how much water was now rushing around us, and how quickly it was rising. I felt anxious as I looked at my son, who was eight years old at the time. Knowing the value of remaining calm, both for my husband who was driving and my son who I did not want to alarm, I quietly said *The Lord's Prayer.* I know the people who were waiting and watching to see whether we would make it through were just as pleased as we were when we finally made it to safety.

That very same week, on a TV show about disasters, I heard reports from survivors and emergency workers who had heard different people saying *The Lord's Prayer* throughout their ordeal—9/11 plane crash victims included. The Lord's Prayer has a basic structure for prayer that covers devotion and a range of prayer needs. Jesus said that it is a prayer that we can say anytime.

~ The Lord's Prayer ~

Our Father, Who art in Heaven,
Hallowed be Thy Name;
Thy Kingdom come,
Thy will be done,
On earth as it is in heaven.
Give us this day our daily bread,
And forgive us our trespasses,
As we forgive those who trespass against us;
And lead us not into temptation,
But deliver us from evil.
(Matthew 6:9–13 and Luke 11:2–4).

Be calm amid insomnia

When I am having trouble falling asleep at night, I find that *The Lord's Prayer* can replace the "pop-ups" that are keeping me awake. The words "forgive us our trespasses, as we forgive others" help with any nagging doubts in my mind; for example, "Oh! I wish I hadn't said or done that." These words also help with any things that have been said or done to me that I have not yet forgiven.

I also say to the racing thoughts, "Be peaceful." This has a sense of command about it that wishy-washy phrases such as "I *wish* I could get to sleep" and "I *wish* I could stop thinking about this" just do not have. I speak firmly to myself: *"Take control, and think as one in control."*

I have suffered from insomnia for many years, and recently, I had three restless nights in a row. The first night, I had three hours of sleep, the second, two hours, and the third, zero. Those who have suffered from this are aware of the frustration of knowing that because you are not sleeping, you are going to suffer from the effects of sleep deprivation the next day. These people will understand that it is rather challenging to remain calm. I tried all the usual remedies, including reading, and I will confess that I did get frustrated with the mystery of why I could not fall asleep on the second night. I calmed the frustration and reassured myself that all would not be lost if I were to rest calmly, as *calm rest is the next best thing to a good night's sleep. I can have a good day after a calm night's rest.* I have come to accept that if insomnia has its way at night, I may need to operate at a slower pace the next day for health and safety reasons, but I can still aspire to have a great day.

It is not only external storms that can affect our calm; we can have trouble remaining calm when we are overtired, overworked, or ill, when the best antidote is just a plain, old time out. We need to be aware on these days that our tolerance levels may be low due to the condition itself, and not necessarily because of a battle with negativity. The Lord knows we will face a variety of battles; he beckons us to trust in his everlasting strength.

> The Lord will give strength to his people; The Lord will bless his people with peace.[xlv]

Be an encourager - All is well

A player was once responsible in the final two minutes of a football game for his team's loss. After the game, he was inconsolable by his teammates. The next morning, he arrived at training in good spirits. When his surprised teammates asked how he could be in such a good mood so soon, he replied, "When my son saw me sad, he asked me, 'what is wrong, dad?' So, I told him, 'I lost the footy, son' and then I just melted when he replied excitedly, 'Don't worry, dad, I will help you find it.'"

King David spoke with encouragement to his soul: "Why are you so downcast, O my soul? Why so disturbed within me? Put your hope in God, for I will yet praise him, my Savior and my God."[xlvi]

Our mind is a thought processor, and there are times when this processing feels like an internal storm. Our grandparents and just about everyone else have taught us to cope with internal storms by speaking seriously to ourselves to reassure ourselves that it will turn out okay; all is well. But how do we convince ourselves that all is well when this may not be the case at that moment? I found the saying "all is well" in a wide range of books used by different writers to encourage readers in their sowing and reaping. Derived from the notion that we reap what we sow, we can see in David's words above that he is talking seriously to himself, choosing to sow the faith that God will come through for him, that all will be well.

Some quote the scripture, "The God who gives life to the dead and calls things that are not as though they were. Against all hope, Abraham in hope believed, and so became the father of many nations"[xlvii]. This hope expressed by Abraham involves a lengthy waiting period, as Abraham and Sarah have their son Isaac when they are well past childbearing age. Abraham and Sarah actually laugh to themselves when they hear that God is going to bless them that year with a child born to Sarah, something they perceive as impossible in their old age.

"Then Abraham fell on his face and laughed and said in his heart, 'Shall a child be born to a man who is one hundred years old? And Sarah who is ninety-nine years old bear a child?'"[xlviii] And the Lord says to Abraham, "Why did Sarah laugh, saying 'shall I surely bear a child since I am old?'"[xlix] This event shows that "With God all things are possible"[l]. We can maintain our calm and peace by trusting that "our Father knows what we need before we ask him"[li]. "For great is his love toward us,"[lii] and "All things work together for good for those who love the Lord"[liii]. We can declare to our storm that God will produce something good out of this; "all is well."

Saint Peter was looking to reap abundant peace for the reader when he wrote the words, "Peace be multiplied"[liv]. What a concept these words hold for us today—a simple phrase we, too, could sow in faith for ourselves, and others.

Peace is faith at rest;
faith that all is well.

Meditate on that which uplifts

One form of meditation is to calmly reflect on something. What we reflect on is our choice. In a letter to the Philippians, Paul suggests that we should meditate on the good to guard our hearts and minds, and he shares a wonderful antidote to negative thinking: "Finally, brethren, whatever things are true, whatever things are noble, whatever things are just, whatever things are pure, whatever things are lovely, whatever things are of good report, if there is any virtue and if there is anything praiseworthy—meditate on these things"[lv].

We are to be rulers of our own minds, and yet, there are days when our minds seem to rule us. If the mind is a tool to be mastered, should we not learn from God in this, the giver of the mind? To gain a greater understanding of any given subject, a scientist will research not only the laws that surround it but also the relevant history and future predictions—our current weather patterns are a good example of this. The Bible is our source for researching God. In it, He has combined the laws that we should live by, parables to give us a greater understanding, history we can learn from, prophesy for our benefit, valuable reminders of His great love for His people, and powerful antidotes for us to meditate on.

Great peace have those who love your law, and nothing causes them to stumble[lvi].

Jesus uses the Scriptures as a response when the devil puts forth his tempting and misguiding advice in the desert after Jesus has fasted for 40 days. With each attack, Jesus opens his reply with, "It is written," referring to the Scriptures of His day. Against the third attack, Jesus says to the devil, "Away with you Satan! For it is written, 'You shall worship the Lord your God, and Him only you shall serve'. Then the devil left him and behold, angels came and ministered to Him"[lvii].

Resist the devil and he will flee from you. Come near to God and he will come near to you[lviii].

Whose hand are you holding?

Satan attempted to cause Jesus to falter in a number of ways; however his attempts achieved nothing but highlight the alliance between Jesus and God. Finding our way in life can sometimes feel like finding our way through a minefield. Every time I face a challenge I ask myself: whose advice is superior, whose words offer encouragement to pursue a divine outcome, and whose hand do I want to hold as I make my way through a potentially explosive situation – Satan's or God's? I will be honest, I don't always recognize the lure of Satan, and feel mortified when I realize I am being influenced by his tainted ways. Nevertheless, when I realign and implement advice that comes from God, the calm and confidence that returns to me is distinctive and inspiring.

Calm & Peace

10

~ ~ ~

~ ~ ~ ~

Content
And Reassured

Calming reassurances of God's love

Uplifting reassurances are important to replace the unloving internal dialogue that can go on in our minds (e.g., "You'll never be good enough"). We can settle our internal storms with antidotes, i.e., reminders to ourselves that we are special to God. We can see from the following words recited by King David that he saw value in speaking positively about his very being: "I will praise You (God), for I am fearfully and wonderfully made"[lix]. King David also assures himself of his security by stating, "Show the great wonder of your great love, you who save by your right hand those who take refuge in you from their foes. Keep me as the apple of your eye"[lx]. A friend once told me that God sings over his people, and I remember thinking, "God sings? Wow, there is something I didn't know, and another reason to feel calm and special." "He will take great delight in you; he will quiet you with his love; he will rejoice over you with singing"[lxi].

God is also interested in the small details of our lives; this can be seen in John's account of Jesus meeting the disciples after they have a hard night of fishing. Although He has a few reasons to meet with them, he meets their immediate basic needs with a warm fire and a hot breakfast. "When the disciples got out of the boat, they saw some bread and a charcoal fire with fish on it."[lxii]

Losing someone or something that we love can leave us in clouds of grief and doubt—a pain we wish would go away; a time when we cry out for help from God, as well as our family and friends. There is a lot of professional advice freely available these days to help with all of the different levels of grief and self-esteem. I have friends, who have prayed and asked God for help through all sorts of experiences, and after doing so, they have made comments to me such as, "I found an inner strength to get me through" or "I had a peace come over me."

> Jesus says, "These things I have spoken to you that in Me you may have peace. In the world you will have tribulation; but be of good cheer, I have overcome the world"[lxiii].

I have found the following personal revelation to be a great antidote in revaluing both myself and others and the treasure we seek. The only treasure Jesus came to pursue on this planet was "us"—a treasure that he was willing to pay for with his life—deeming "us" a priceless treasure.

No pity parties

Pity parties are little group gatherings where one or more of the people gathered are engaged in telling a stream of "poor me" stories and expressing fear that things will never change. I do not enjoy pity parties, let alone discovering that I have inadvertently become the leader of one. "Poor me" stories are sometimes born out of discontentment. However, we should take comfort at such times, as we all have the ability to strengthen our inner contentment and reduce our natural ability to complain. Paul openly shares his own *learning* process for contentment as follows: "I have learned in whatever state I am, to be content"[lxiv]. Remaining calm and content is something that we, too, can learn.

I mentioned at the beginning of this book that I was forced to learn about anxiety due to the onset of heart palpitations. For a while, I added to my own stress levels with my fears about the condition. One night over dinner, I was telling some very dear friends that my father had suffered a similar nervous condition, and as his condition never seemed to improve, mine may not either, for genetic reasons. Look at those words closely—oh, how they lack any encouragement for improvement! What an excuse they are for giving up! My friends recited these great words to me: "For God has not given us a spirit of fear, but of power, love, and a sound mind"[lxv]. These were life-changing words for me, and I am no longer content with fearing whether or not I suffer from an inherited condition; I choose now to learn how I can better connect with God's gift of His power, love, and sound thinking.

I find that there are just as many questions as there are answers to achieving contentment, as there are things that we should be content with and things that we should not, there are things that we can change and things that we cannot. For some reason, I feel a peace and contentment come over me that is hard to explain whenever I state, "I will be content because God is with me, whether I am sensing his presence or not, whether I am in a banquet with all those I love or at home alone eating dry bread." I believe that God desires us to see Him as the treasure that He sees us to be. Those who treasure the companionship of the Lord find reassurance in the following scripture.

For the Lord your God, He is the One who goes with you. He will not leave you nor forsake you.[lxvi]

11

~~~

~~~~

A Valuable Contribution

The wise stand strong to help restore peace,
while the faint-hearted deem it impossible

We can easily let life's frustrations and petty grievances disturb our calm and peace anywhere, but I would like to suggest that home is a good place to practice our response to turmoil. Moreover, the home is a very fitting place to enthusiastically contribute valuable calm and peace.

It never ceases to surprise me, the many and varied ways that turmoil can rear its ugly head, either within my thoughts or in external occurrences. I can say with utmost sincerity that I can increasingly see the value of the time and energy I have invested in learning God's calm and peaceful ways.

God teaches that his people can mature with an inner peace that resembles His true righteousness and holiness. Ephesians 4 of the Christian Bible suggests that a valuable element of this teaching is to renew our attitude, evaluate who we are and how we react, identify and reject the thoughts and attitudes tainted with Satan's influence, that is, give Satan no foothold at all, and instead, embrace and highly value growing as a person and interconnecting with God's Spirit of love and peace.

Being at peace with others

It is not uncommon for good relationships to disintegrate due to adverse reactions to situations; furthermore, bad feelings can continue long after the original turmoil is over. Adverse reactions, like thorns, are better dealt with the moment we feel the pain. Also like thorns, lingering bad feelings are not always visible; yet we know something is inside and festering. When one neglects to deal with bad feelings, he or she is like a bear that picks up a few thorns in his paw and continues walking, wondering why he is feeling uncomfortable and grumpy. Dealing with our reactions and feelings may take strength, but whenever we use our strength, we grow in strength.

It takes training for a police officer to stay calm while exerting firm authority to break up a fight. As we train ourselves to grow strong in the ways of calmness and peace, we are not only a help to ourselves but to those around us through our example. We know not where or when we or those close to us may need to rise up and deal with turmoil and adverse reactions, but these are the moments when acquired wisdom and training help those involved to be strong like a bear, but a bear that is in control.

Sharing peace in our society

In an act of reconciliation, Yehudi Menuhin, an internationally renowned violinist, became one of the first Jewish musicians to perform in Germany after the Holocaust. He shares the value he placed on peace as follows.

> Peace may sound simple—one beautiful word—but it requires everything we have, every quality, every strength, every dream, every high ideal (Yehudi Menuhin, 1916–1999).[11]

I know I often feel like running from or complaining bitterly about turmoil. It is during these moments that I remind myself that calm and peace are highly valued gems that we all seek and spoken by Jesus to come with a blessing. Matthew 5: 9: "blessed are the peace makers."

The old saying, "prevention is better than a cure" is true for storms that can be prevented by the intervention of peace. Many listened to Martin Luther

---

[11] wagingpeace.org/menu/issues/peace-&-war/start/peace-quotes/index.htm.

Calm & Peace

King Jr. (1929–1968) in the 1950s and 60s, and many still reflect on his speeches today. He spoke of the importance of a peaceful and non-violent society. His "Six Principles and Steps to Non-Violent Social Change" can be found on the Internet,[12] and are as relevant today as they were then. I have chosen two of these to share with you:

> Principle 5: Non-violence chooses loving solutions, not hateful ones.
>
> Step 4: Peacefully negotiate; talk with both sides. Go to the people in your community who are in trouble and who are deeply hurt by society's ills. Also go to those people who are contributing to the breakdown of a peaceful society. Use humor, intelligence, and grace to lead to solutions that benefit the greater good.

A modern day example of these principles in action is embodied in an Australian woman, Gillian Hicks, who survived the July 2005 London bombing. Standing mere feet away from the suicide bomber, Gillian was

---

[12] cpt.org/files/PW%20-%20Principles%20-%20King.pdf.

severely and permanently injured, losing both her legs from the knees down. She has an immeasurable depth of gratitude to those who did everything they could to save her life. She is determined to make her life count and is spreading a message of peace via her website, madnests.com M.A.D.—(Making A Difference) for peace. Her web statement suggests the following: Peace starts within the very heart of each and every one of us.

> The work of one person can make a significant difference, but the combined work of several / many people is very powerful and can create lasting positive change.

The University of Colorado at Boulder has set up a fabulous website[13] that offers a free knowledge base of more constructive approaches to destructive conflict. It is easy to love those who are near and dear to us, but world peace must include all men and women.

---

[13] beyondintractability.org.

If it is possible, as much as it depends on you, live peaceably with all men.[lxvii]

As a society, we can share the antidotes that help us maintain calm and peace—antidotes that build each other and ourselves up. I read recently that there has been a resurgence of interest in the 900-year-old writings of St. Francis of Assisi, an Italian friar who founded the Franciscan order of monks. The most widely recognized of these writings is his Peace Prayer. I have seen this prayer mounted, framed, and hanging proudly on many a wall.

In March 2013 Cardinal Jorge Mario Bergoglio was elected the 266th Pope of the Catholic Church. He chose the name Francis to honor St. Francis of Assisi and to prompt himself to remember the saint's values; this choice has been applauded worldwide.

~ Peace Prayer ~

Lord, make me an instrument of your peace,
Where there is hatred, let me sow love;
Where there is injury, pardon;
Where there is doubt, faith;
Where there is despair, hope;
Where there is darkness, light;
And where there is sadness, joy;
O Lord - Grant that I may not so much seek
To be consoled as to console;
To be understood, as to understand;
To be loved as to love;
For it is in giving that we receive,
It is in pardoning that we are pardoned,
And it is in dying
That we are born to eternal life

(St. Francis of Assisi, 1181–1226).[14]

---

[14] fmm.org.au/water/francis.htm.

It cannot be left unsaid that many have endured the opposite of calm and peace when standing up for calm and peace. Incredible sacrifices have been made for the benefit of others. For many, this has been the ultimate sacrifice—their own lives cut short on the battlefield, fighting to restore peace in a country—while others have been martyred for their beliefs. Jesus warns us that those who live for the betterment of His peace will encounter division from those who do not. He also says that the smallest seed can grow into the largest tree. In this wonderful age of documentation, we can review stories, from major battles in history to personal stories from people of all walks of life who have made a valuable contribution to peace—stories that show us that victory is never far off for those who plant seeds of peace.

In making peace, a crucial element when facing adversaries is to help restore dignity to all involved. Nelson Mandela was jailed for 27 years in his own country of South Africa. His crime was a desire to see blacks and whites living peacefully side-by-side, as equals.

It always seems impossible until it is done! Man's goodness is a flame that can be hidden, but never extinguished (Nelson Mandela 1918–).

Whether it is a reported event shown on television or an experience within our friends and families, it is uplifting to see man's goodness in action, a goodness that inspires others to ignite a flame for peace.

Value perseverance

The pains that I experienced with heart palpitations may have initially assisted in driving my motivation to adopt God's calm and peaceful way of thinking, but I am very happy with the joy I have come to experience from learning how to persevere. Perseverance rewards those who know that good results are worth working toward in spite of difficulties.

By perseverance the snail reached the ark! (Charles Haddon Spurgeon, 1834–1892. Spurgeon was a well-known preacher in London during the nineteenth century).[15]

---

[15] quotationspage.com/subjects/perseverance/.

A strong passion for calm and peace can assist our perseverance—a passion that comes to our rescue when we flare up; a passion that fights our own justifications and strong will; a passion that insists that two wrongs don't make a right; a passion that looks for what needs to be done in order for calm and peace to prevail.

Where calm and peace prevail
Joy and happiness flourish.

Jesus' calm and peaceful yet strong and determined attitude assisted Him through the storm of the cross to take his place at the right hand of God the Father. Through this act, He could offer renewed access to God to the billions of people on the planet—a joy and happiness that are intended to flourish for eternity.

Now may the Lord of peace Himself give you peace always in every way. The Lord *be* with you all.[lxviii]

Calm & Peace

~ *Footnote* ~

"The pen is mightier than the sword."

I have added a few pages here for you to pen that which you have found in your life helps you overcome turmoil, that is, antidotes that help maintain your calm and peace.

Wisdom cherished and documented is wisdom
that lives on long after the memory has faded.
Wisdom that is shared can live on in the
hearts and minds of generations to come.

Adrina Green

Calm & Peace

~~~ *Notes* ~~~

~~~ *Notes* ~~~

~~~ *Notes* ~~~

Calm & Peace

~~~ Notes ~~~

~~~ *Notes* ~~~

~~~ Notes ~~~

References

---

[i] NKJV Luke 2:14
[ii] NIV Proverbs18:14
[iii] NIV Proverbs 19:8
[iv] KNJV Proverbs 17:27
[v] NIV Genesis 2:17
[vi] NKJV Genesis 3:4,5
[vii] NIV John 14:26
[viii] NIV Revelation 12:9
[ix] NIV Ephesians 6:11
[x] NIV Psalm 94: 18,19
[xi] CEV 2 Chronicles 1:7–12
[xii] KNJV 1 Kings 10:7,8
[xiii] NIV James 3:16
[xiv] NIV Genesis 4:6
[xv] NKJV Psalm 34:14
[xvi] NIV James 3:4–6
[xvii] GNB James 3:18
[xviii] NKJV Proverbs 17:22
[xix] NIV Psalm23
[xx] KNJV Proverbs 15:24
[xxi] GNB Proverbs 4:23
[xxii] NKJV Exodus 20:17
[xxiii] GNB Matthew 16:21
[xxiv] KNJV Matthew 1:23
[xxv] NIV Isaiah 53:2
[xxvi] NIV Matthew 4:6
[xxvii] NIV Mark 8:11,12
[xxviii] NIV Matthew 26:53,54
[xxix] NKJV Mark 15:3,4
[xxx] NKJV John 10:17,18
[xxxi] NKJV Mark 10:45

[xxxii] NIV Luke 23:34
[xxxiii] NIV 1 John 4:18
[xxxiv] CEV 1 Corinthians 13:3–6
[xxxv] GNB Proverbs 14:30
[xxxvi] NIV Deuteronomy 33:25–27
[xxxvii] NIV Isaiah 40:31
[xxxviii] NKJV 2 Chronicles 16:9
[xxxix] NIV Isaiah 41:10
[xl] NIV John 3:16
[xli] NKJV John 14:26,27
[xlii] NIV Hebrews 2:14–18
[xliii] NKJV Romans 10:9
[xliv] NKJV Romans 5:5
[xlv] NKJV Psalm 29:11
[xlvi] NIV Psalm 43:5
[xlvii] NIV Romans 4:17,18
[xlviii] NKJV Genesis 17:17
[xlix] NKJV Genesis 18:13
[l] NKJV Matthew 19:26
[li] NIV Matthew 6:8
[lii] NIV Psalm 117:2
[liii] NKJV Romans 8:28
[liv] NKJV 1 Peter 1:2
[lv] NKJ Phil 4:8
[lvi] NKJV Psalm 119:165
[lvii] NKJV Matthew 4: 10,11
[lviii] NIV James 4:7
[lix] NKJV Psalm 139:14
[lx] NIV Psalm 17:7,8
[lxi] NIV Zephaniah 3:17
[lxii] GNB John 21:9
[lxiii] NKJV John 16:33
[lxiv] NKJV Philippians 4:11
[lxv] NKJV 2Timothy 1:7
[lxvi] NKJV Deuteronomy 31:6
[lxvii] NKJV Romans 12:18.
[lxviii] NKJV 2 Thessalonians 3:16.

Calm & Peace

---

www.ingramcontent.com/pod-product-compliance
Lightning Source LLC
Chambersburg PA
CBHW021159020426
42331CB00003B/126